A JOURNAL

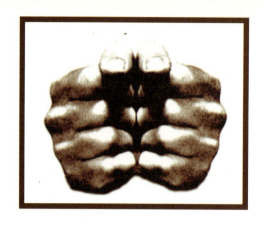

"A UNIQUE TRADITION, OUTSIDE ALL CONCEPTS, WITH NO DEPENDENCE ON WORDS; POINTING DIRECTLY AT TRUE WISDOM!"

THESE WORDS BY BODHIDHARMA, 1,300 YEARS AGO, SIGNALED THE COMING OF INDIAN BUDDHISM INTO CHINA AND THE CREATION OF CHAN BUDDHISM. CHAN TRAVELED TO JAPAN AND ZEN WAS BORN. NOW ZEN HAS COME TO THE WESTERN WORLD AND AMERICAN ZEN IS BORN. AS CULTURES MEET AND COLLIDE, UNPREDICTABLE CHANGES OCCUR; WISDOM EMERGES.

WORDS BY DOGEN, SHUNRYU SUZUKI AND OTHERS MEET THE PLAYFUL, POWERFUL IMAGES OF MICHAEL GREEN TO PROVIDE WAKE-UP CALLS TO OUR TRUE AND NATURAL WISDOM.

"THE SECRET OF ZEN IS JUST TWO WORDS - NOT ALWAYS SO!"
—SHUNRYU SUZUKI

THE SPIRIT OF THIS QUOTE CAPTURES THE MYSTERIOUS, PROFOUND, HUMOROUS AND PARADOXICAL NATURE THAT IS AMERICAN ZEN™.

IN ZEN PRACTICE THERE IS AN EXPRESSION, "WHEN WE ARE TRULY OURSELVES, THEN ZEN IS ZEN." JOURNAL WRITING IS AS MUCH A MEANS TO THE DISCOVERY OF OUR TRUE SELF AS IN ZEN PRACTICE IS THE PRACTICE OF MEDITATION. WHETHER WE ARE PRACTICING JOURNALING OR MEDITATION, WE AIM TO GO BEYOND OUR ORDINARY WAY OF VIEWING OURSELVES AND THE WORLD, AND WE BEGIN TO UNDERSTAND AND APPRECIATE THE JOURNEY. ENJOY THE PATH, GO BEYOND THE USUAL AND PERHAPS DISCOVER SOMETHING THAT YOU KNOW, OR DON'T KNOW -

"IF YOU CANNOT FIND THE TRUTH RIGHT WHERE YOU ARE, WHERE DO YOU EXPECT TO FIND IT?"
—DOGEN

IF YOU CANNOT FIND THE TRUTH
RIGHT WHERE YOU ARE,
WHERE DO YOU EXPECT TO FIND IT?

-DOGEN

In this house there

are no signal drums.

When dust settles,

There's the broom!

Past mind can't be grasped.

Present mind
can't be grasped.

Future mind
can't be
grasped.

THIS is a light abounding in full gladness, like coming upon a light in thick darkness, like receiving treasure in poverty. So easy, so free are you, that the weight of the world and the aggravations of the mind are burdens no longer; your existence is delivered from all limitations. You have become open, light and transparent. You gain an illuminating insight into the deepest nature of things, which appear to you as so many gossamer patterns having no graspable reality! Here is the original face of your being. Here is the straight passage, open and unobstructed. Here is where you surrender all. This is where you gain peace, ease, non-doing and inexpressible delight. All sutras and scriptures are not more than communications of this fact. All the sages, ancient and modern, have exhausted their ingenuity and imaginations to no other purpose than to point the way to **THIS**.

THE SECRET OF ZEN IS JUST TWO WORDS:
NOT ALWAYS SO!

–SHUNRYU SUZUKI

THE ROSE DOES
BEST AS A ROSE. LILIES
MAKE THE BEST LILIES.
AND LOOK–
  YOU!
THE BEST YOU AROUND!

LAST NIGHT I DREAMT I WAS A
BUTTERFLY. TODAY,
...AM I A BUTTERFLY DREAMING
I AM A MAN?

        – CHUANG YZU

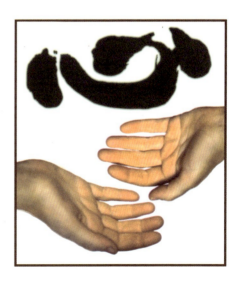

THE WORLD IS ITS OWN MAGIC.

   -SHUNRYU SUZUKI

PINE CONE ZEN

WITH A
CALM MIND

HAPPINESS ARISES.

THE EARTH
IS SUPPORTED,
BY A PINE CONE.

TRY NOT TO ACHIEVE ANYTHING SPECIAL

AS LONG AS YOU SEEK FOR "SOMETHING,"
YOU WILL GET THE SHADOW OF REALITY,
NOT REALITY ITSELF.

-SHUNRYU SUZUKI

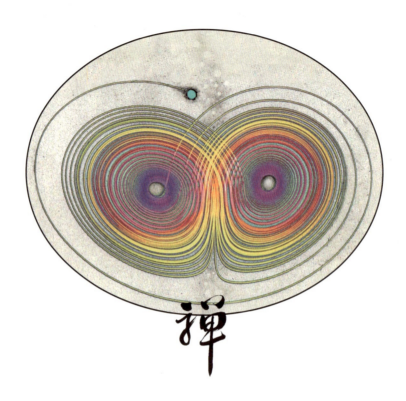

O<small>N ONE SIDE WE
ARE ALL FOOLS.</small>

BUT

WHEN WE REALIZE THIS,
WE ARE ENLIGHTENED.
-SHUNRYU SUZUKI

BE GRATEFUL FOR WHOEVER COMES,
BECAUSE EACH HAS BEEN SENT
AS A GUIDE FROM BEYOND.

-RUMI

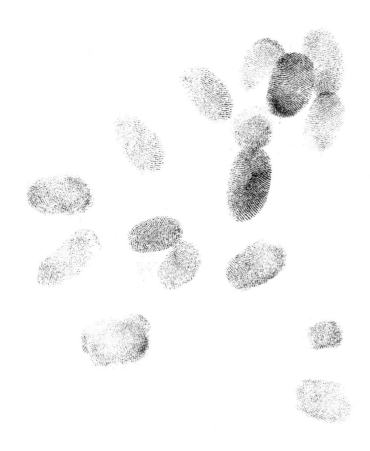
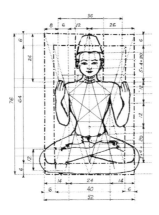

WHAT IS THE SHAPE OF MY LIFE?
WHAT IS THE SOUND OF RAIN?

SIT LIKE A MOUNTAIN

MOVE LIKE A RIVER,

SHINE LIKE THE SUN!

THE EMPEROR ASKS BODHIDHARMA

"...WHAT IS THE FIRST
PRINCIPLE OF HOLINESS?"

BODHIDHARMA REPLIES:

VASTNESS!

...NO HOLINESS.

> TO STUDY THE WAY
> IS TO STUDY THE
> SELF.
>
> TO STUDY THE SELF
> IS TO FORGET THE
> SELF.
>
> TO FORGET THE
> SELF
>
> IS TO BE
> AWAKENED
>
> WITH ALL THINGS
>
> —DOGEN

the
Buddha

said:

"There is a
turning
around

we must accomplish."

IT MAKES JUST ABOUT NO DIFFERENCE WHAT PEOPLE THINK OF YOU!

AS IS
THE GARDENER

SUCH IS THE
GARDEN

-HEBREW PROVERB

The American Zen journal can be traced to artist and cross-cultural drifter, Michael Green. Also responsible for ZEN & THE ART OF THE MACINTOSH, THE ILLUMINATED RUMI and a variety of other books. Michael has done a tour in film-school, hitch-hiked through the Amazon, lived in tipis, painted signs and studied ten years with Sufi master Bawa Muhaiyaddeen. He is now working on Millennium Sutra, a major museum installation.

Brush Dance

A Journal with the art of Michael Green. Copyright © 2001 published by Brush Dance. All rights reserved. No part of this book may be reproduced or transmitted in any form or by any means, electronic or mechanical, including photocopying, recording, or by any information storage and retrieval system, without written permission from the publisher.

A special thanks to the San Francisco Zen center for permission to print quotations by Shunryu Suzuki.

The Master* was asked,
"What time is it?"
He replied,

Do you mean NOW?